P9-CCE-939

ROSH HASHANAH
AND
YOM KIPPUR

Text copyright © 1979 by Howard Greenfeld
Illustrations copyright © 1979 by Elaine Grove
Published simultaneously in Canada by Holt, Rinehart
and Winston of Canada, Limited.
Printed in the United States of America
10 9 8 7 6 5 4 3 2 1

Library of Congress Cataloging in Publication Data

Greenfeld, Howard.   Rosh Hashanah and Yom Kippur.

SUMMARY: Discusses the meaning, history, and
observance of Rosh Hashanah and Yom Kippur.
1. High Holy Days — Juvenile literature. [1. Rosh
ha-Shanah. 2. Yom Kippur. 3. Fasts and feasts —
Judaism] I. Grove, Elaine. II. Title.
BM693.H5G735   296.4'31   79-4818   ISBN 0-03-044756-9

by
HOWARD GREENFELD

---

illustrated by
ELAINE GROVE

Holt, Rinehart and Winston
New York

Rosh Hashanah and Yom Kippur are the most intensely religious days in the Jewish calendar; together they are known as the High Holy Days. On these most holy and most solemn days of the year, Jews all over the world spend their time in the synagogue, where they devote many hours to self-examination and prayer. Recognizing the vital presence of God in their lives, they confess to sins committed in the past, and they ask forgiveness by pledging to correct these sins and by resolving to improve their ways in the future.

These profoundly serious holidays are truly holy days — religious days — and their celebration is marked by reflection on the moral responsibility of man and his all-important relationship to God.

They are the most important of all Jewish holidays and also probably the least understood, for neither Rosh Hashanah nor Yom Kippur deal with easily explained historical events (as do Passover and Chanukah) or with seasonal celebrations (as do Sukkoth and Shavuot). There is no "story" connected with them. Instead, they are concerned solely with complicated abstract ideas, such as "sin," "repentance," "redemption," "man's relationship to God," and "man's moral responsibilities." The meaning behind these holidays is, therefore, not simple to understand, yet understanding is of great importance, for these holidays, more than any others, embody the unique experience and the values of being a Jew.

5

6

ROSH HASHANAH

The first of these most holy days is called Rosh Hashanah — Hebrew words meaning "head of the year" or new year. This Jewish new year, celebrated each fall, is not a time of noisy celebration, marked by loud, cheerful cries. It is, instead, the start of a sober, solemn ten-day period of contemplation and self-examination, a period which begins with Rosh Hashanah and ends with Yom Kippur, the second of the High Holy Days. It is a period of reverence and of prayer, when Jews are called upon to give an account of their behavior to the community and to God, a time when they repent of their own sins and pray not only for their own redemption but for the well-being of the entire world.

Though the holiday is not celebrated joyously as are so many other new year celebrations, the element of joy is not entirely missing; joy as well as gratitude for the good things of the past year are a part of the festival. However, this is a thoughtful joy, tempered by meditation on the uncertainties of the future. At this time, in the words of a Psalm, Jews "rejoice with trembling."

More than just the beginning of the religious year for Jews, Rosh Hashanah celebrates the day on which the world was

9

created. This anniversary of creation is also called the Day of Remembrance. According to tradition, on this day God reviews the deeds of all mankind during the past year. To achieve His judgment, three books are opened in heaven. In one will be written the names of all those who have been entirely virtuous during the past year; the second contains the names of those who have been entirely evil; and in the third book are inscribed the names of those who have been neither completely wicked nor completely virtuous.

The entirely virtuous are immediately written in the book of life, assuring life in the coming year, while the entirely wicked are inscribed in the book of death. The fate of the third group — and the large majority of all people falls into this group — is kept in suspension until Yom Kippur, which ends the High Holy Days. In this ten-day period between Rosh Hashanah and Yom Kippur Jews repent their sins, pray that they will be forgiven, and correct their ways by performing good acts so that they might finally be inscribed in the book of life when, on Yom Kippur, the books are sealed for the coming year.

These themes — recognition of God as the universal judge, sincere regrets for past

11

wrongdoings, penitence, and hope for the future—dominate the celebration of Rosh Hashanah.

On the eve of the holiday, a festive meal is served in the home. It is much like any other holiday meal, but there are a few differences to set it apart. Hallah, the white bread eaten on each Sabbath evening, is usually baked in a long, braided loaf. For Rosh Hashanah, it comes in a variety of different shapes. It is round rather than long, its roundness symbolizing the hope for a full year and a long life. Sometimes there is a small ladder on top of the loaf, for God judges who will ascend and who will descend. Sometimes a decorative bird is placed on top of the loaf, so that our prayers might fly off to heaven. Other loaves have braided crowns around them, a reminder that God is our king, our ruler.

After a piece of this bread has been blessed by the father of the family, it is not merely passed around the table, as on the Sabbath; it is first dipped in honey, with the wish that the new year might be as sweet as honey. For the same reason, a slice of seasonal fruit, usually an apple, is also dipped in honey and blessed before it is eaten.

Once the dinner is concluded, the family goes to the synagogue, for Rosh

13

Hashanah is celebrated in the house of worship. The rabbi and the cantor are dressed in white; the curtains of the ark, too, are white, as is the covering for the scrolls of the Torah, for white is the symbol of purity and forgiveness, the color of the High Holy Days. Throughout the service, the congregation prays for a good new year. When the service comes to an end, the members of the congregation leave the synagogue full of hope that a compassionate God has heard their prayers. Friends and family are greeted with the words: "May you be inscribed in the book of life for a good year."

The following morning, the religious services are continued in the synagogue. These services contain some of the most profound concepts of Judaism. These are beautifully expressed through ancient prayers, selections from the Bible, the Talmud, and many works of Hebrew literature, both classical and modern. All are found in the *Mahzor,* the special book of prayers used on the High Holy Days.

Among these prayers, one that movingly describes Rosh Hashanah as the day of God's judgment begins with the words: "We will declare the greatness of this day." It states that on this day all creatures

לשנה טובה תכתבו

15

pass before God, who decrees their fate. And it speaks of God's mercy and capacity for forgiveness, since "repentance, prayer, and charity avert the final decree." This belief, fundamental to Rosh Hashanah, confirms that those who have sinned still have the chance to be forgiven before being condemned to the book of death.

Another prayer embodies other important ideas of this holy day:

Remember us for life,
King, who delights in life,
And inscribe us
In the book of life.

"Remember" refers to this holiday as the Day of Remembrance, when God remembers the deeds of man. "King" is a reminder of the eternal sovereignty of God, and the plea to be inscribed in the book of life refers to the final judgment.

Still another prayer begins with the words, "Our Father, our King, we have sinned before you." God is thus recognized as both the compassionate father and the awesome king, and before Him the celebrants recognize that they have sinned and plead for mercy and understanding.

All of these inspiring prayers combine to create a feeling of extreme piety on the

17

morning of Rosh Hashanah, but perhaps the most dramatic and stirring moments of the entire ritual come with the blowing of the trumpet-like instrument called the shofar.

The shofar is one of the oldest of all musical instruments still in use today. It is also one of the simplest, for it consists solely of the curved and hollowed horn of an animal, through which a series of musical notes is blown. For use on Rosh Hashanah and later on Yom Kippur, the shofar cannot be artificially manufactured. It must be naturally hollow and naturally curved, the curve symbolizing man's sub-

servience to God. Though the horn of any one of a number of animals would be acceptable, it is the horn of a ram that is traditionally used for the High Holy Days; for it is a reminder of the story of Abraham, who, out of his love for God, was prepared to sacrifice his only son Isaac, but was permitted by an understanding God to sacrifice a ram in the place of his son. This story is, appropriately, recounted during the Rosh Hashanah service.

This ancient instrument has played a significant part in the history of the Jews. It was formerly used to sound an alarm with loud, sudden blasts and also to declare war;

19

it was also used to announce holidays and to signal the appearance of the new moon. In modern times, however, it is blown only on the High Holy Days. It announces the start of these holidays, and it is also a reminder of glorious moments in the history of the Jews. In the Bible it is written that the Torah was given to Israel with the sound of the shofar, and that Israel won the battle of Jericho to the accompaniment of the shofar's blast. It is also a clarion call to conscience, a signal to stop and think of the way we have led and lead our lives. On the morning of Rosh Hashanah, it reminds all Jews that God is the ruler and the judge of the universe, that judgment will soon be made. It is a cry for spiritual renewal.

The haunting sounds of the shofar are heard at a few points during this service for the new year. Each time, Jews are reminded of the holiness of this occasion, and when the notes of the shofar are sounded toward the end of the Rosh Hashanah service and the members of the congregation again wish one another inscription in the book of life, they understand that they are called to judgment not so that they might be punished, but rather so that they might renounce their sins in favor of a virtuous way of life.

YOM KIPPUR

Yom Kippur, the Day of Atonement, is referred to as the Sabbath of Sabbaths; it is the holiest day of the Jewish year. On this day, God considers and weighs the deeds of all mankind.

Forgiveness for sin is the principal theme of Yom Kippur. God is merciful and will forgive those who sincerely repent, for sin is a human weakness that can be overcome by repentance, prayer, and charity. Yom Kippur, then, is also an annual rebirth, for Jews gain a new spiritual life through the inner peace achieved by repentance.

Before Jews can be forgiven for those sins committed against God, they must seek and obtain the pardon of those whom they have wronged throughout the year. Before Yom Kippur, all disputes must be settled; wrongs committed against others must be confessed, and forgiveness must be granted by those who have been harmed. At the same time, all Jews must themselves be forgiving and must not seek revenge against any who might have wronged them or carry any lingering malice. A merciful God demands mercy of them before He will listen to their prayers.

This day of atonement, of final judgment, is also a day of self-affliction, a day on which no work may be done and a day

23

of complete fasting. From sunset on the eve of Yom Kippur to sunset the following day, there is to be no eating and no drinking.

As the families of the community enter a synagogue, there is a hushed air of piety. The last meal before the fast is over; the celebrants have eaten heartily and well, but they have been careful not to eat foods that could make them thirsty — for even a glass of water is forbidden under the laws of their religion. Until the following evening, all thought must be directed toward prayer.

The aged and sick, who could suffer from fasting, are exempted from fasting, as are young children. Traditionally, no child under the age of nine is permitted to fast for even a part of the day, since it might be harmful to his or her health. By the age of nine, a child may gradually begin to fast. At first, this might mean postponing a meal for an hour or two; later it could mean eliminating a customary snack or either breakfast or lunch. A child of thirteen joins the adult community. He or she participates in the day-long fast and spends Yom Kippur in the synagogue, absorbed in self-examination and prayer.

Near the beginning of the service on this Yom Kippur eve comes one of the most moving times in the religious life of the Jew.

25

The white curtains are drawn from the ark, the congregation rises, the Torah scrolls are taken out, and the white-robed cantor begins to chant the *Kol Nidrei*. This prayer (*kol nidrei* can be translated from the Hebrew as "all vows") is a proclamation that all personal vows made hastily, impulsively, or without thought during the year should be annulled. This declaration has, throughout history, been used by anti-Semites against the Jews, as evidence that the word of a Jew is meaningless. This, however, is a deliberate misinterpretation of a declaration that does not include vows made between persons; it refers only to vows made between a Jew and God. The purpose of the *Kol Nidrei* proclamation is to forgive those — and tragically there have been many of them — who throughout history have, under threat of torture or death, been forced to renounce the Jewish religion and accept another faith. Nonetheless, this prayer is, in some synagogues, replaced today by Psalm 130, a plaintive plea for redemption. Whatever the words, however, the melody of the *Kol Nidrei*, which is most probably of sixteenth-century South German origin, speaks to the hearts of all Jews. Chanted three times by the cantor, it seems to cry out for forgiveness, compassion, and mercy.

27

Later in the evening service another of the great prayers of the High Holy Days is recited, an all-encompassing confession, the first words of each line beginning with "For the sin we have sinned against Thee." Every possible sin that might have been committed during the past year is named. Slander, arrogance, dishonesty, disrespect, stubbornness, exploitation, and treachery are only a few, since this is a collective confession, a plea for pardon not for the individual but for all peoples.

Toward the end of the service, the prayer first recited on Rosh Hashanah, "Our Father, our King" is repeated, a reaffirmation of the sovereignty and mercy of God.

The following day, which pious Jews devote entirely to prayer and meditation, both of these prayers are among the many prayers, poems, and Psalms that are chanted or recited in the synagogue. Throughout this most sacred of days, there are repeated confessions of wrongdoing and pleas for mercy and understanding, just as there are promises to right these wrongs and lead a virtuous life in the year to come.

Toward late afternoon, portions of the Book of Jonah are read. This story is of

29

particular significance on Yom Kippur, because it shows the value of true repentance and teaches that God's mercy extends to all who repent.

Shortly afterward, the afternoon service comes to an end. It is followed by a memorial service, during which the dead are remembered with blessings and love.

The appearance of the first three stars in the sky signals the day's end. Finally, there comes the *Ne'ilah*, the concluding service of the High Holy Days. *Ne'ilah* is the Hebrew word for "closing," and this is literally the closing service, for at this time the gates of heaven, of mercy, are closed. It is the last chance for repentance and for forgiveness,

and the final prayer, "May we enter Thy gates," expresses the wish to be received by God in mercy and to be sealed in the book of life.

A long, single blast of the shofar is sounded.

The Sabbath of Sabbaths comes to an end.

Feeling purified, the observant Jew continues his life.

For many, as an affirmation, the first task upon leaving the synagogue will be to put up the framework of the *sukkah*, the booth or shelter that is the symbol of the joyous holiday of Sukkoth which comes four days after Yom Kippur and celebrates the reaping of the harvest.

31